The Glorious American

→ SONGBOOK ←

To the memory of Dale Evans and Roy Rogers

Book design by Susan Van Horn.
Typeset in Stempel Schneidler and Old Claud.
Music engraving by Robert Puff, RPM Seattle Music Preparation, www.musicprep.com.
Manufactured in China.
ISBN 0-8118-4552-4

Distributed in Canada by Raincoast Books
9050 Shaughnessy Street, Vancouver, British Columbia V6P 6E5

10 9 8 7 6 5 4 3 2 1

Chronicle Books LLC
85 Second Street, San Francisco, California 94105

www.chroniclekids.com

The Glorious American
→ SONGBOOK ←

A CLASSIC ILLUSTRATED EDITION

Compiled by Cooper Edens

chronicle books · san francisco

PREFACE

Over the years, heartfelt American ingenuity has blended diverse styles of music with many surprising results. Colonial-era music was originally that of the settlers' homelands—but as the new country was forged, and as immigrants arrived from more and more countries, a new music began to develop. On the frontier, new themes emerged to fit the new situations. Out of the close association of people from widely varied backgrounds grew our county's precious musical sound, which had never been heard before and could only have been created in America. Such typically American musical forms as square-dance music, cowboy songs, and gospel hymns are examples of the merging of the dance, ballad, and religious traditions of different cultures. The importance of the contributions of Africans brought here as slaves cannot be overestimated, for their joyous and complex melodic, harmonic, and rhythmic influence made possible folk, blues, bluegrass, country, ragtime, and jazz.

America's glorious songbook is as varied as her landscapes and peoples, and the many faces of American song reflect musical influences from all over the world. The songs in this book paint a portrait of the people who made America great: her pioneers, railroad workers, gold miners, farmers, traveling musicians, hobos, soldiers, sailors, tradespeople, patriots, lovers, church-goers, and slaves.

Since this country was founded, homemade music has been an important part of its rich tradition. So sing along! Many of the songs in *The Glorious American Songbook* are so common that every child will know them. They are gathered here for you to celebrate our common heritage.

Our greatest songs are yet unsung. Perhaps you will write the next glorious one!

—*Cooper Edens*

TABLE OF CONTENTS

Don't Fence Me In

BY COLE PORTER (1944)

Cole Porter, one of America's greatest composers, and a stylish
easterner, wrote of his love of the West.

Oh, give me land, lots of land under starry skies above,
Don't fence me in.
Let me ride through the wide open country that I love,
Don't fence me in.

Let me be by myself in the evening breeze,
Listen to the murmur of the cottonwood trees.
Send me off forever, but I ask you please,
Don't fence me in.

Just turn me loose. Let me straddle my old saddle underneath the
     western skies.
On my Cayuse, let me wander over yonder till I see the
     mountains rise.
I want to ride to the ridge where the West commences,
Gaze at the moon till I lose my senses,
Can't look at hobbles and I can't stand fences,
Don't fence me in.

Oh, give me land, lots of land un-der star-ry skies a-bove, Don't fence me in

Let me ride thru the wide o-pen coun-try that I love, Don't fence me in.

Oh, Susanna!

BY STEPHEN FOSTER (1847)

Stephen Foster once wrote that the little money he received from
"Oh, Susanna!" was enough to get him started as a songwriter.

I come from Alabama with a banjo on my knee;
I'm going to Louisiana, my Susanna for to see.
It rained all night the day I left, the weather it was dry;
The sun so hot I froze to death, Susanna, don't you cry.

Oh, Susanna! Don't you cry for me,
For I come from Alabama with a banjo on my knee.

I had a dream the other night, when everything was still;
I thought I saw Susanna come a-walking down the hill,
A red, red rose was in her cheek, a tear was in her eye;
I said to her, "Susanna, girl, Susanna, don't you cry."

Oh, Susanna! Don't you cry for me,
For I come from Alabama with a banjo on my knee.

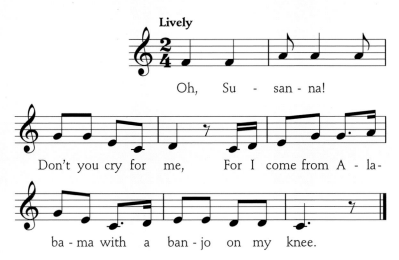

Buffalo Gals

BY COOL WHITE (1844)

Cool White, a minstrel singer, wrote this dance tune in 1844. It's about the women of Buffalo, Pittsburgh, Charleston—or wherever White's band happened to be playing. Mark Twain used the song in Tom Sawyer.

Buffalo gals, won't you come out tonight?
Come out tonight? Come out tonight?
Buffalo gals, won't you come out tonight
And dance by the light of the moon?

Oh, yes, pretty boys, we're coming out tonight,
Coming out tonight, coming out tonight.
Oh, yes, pretty boys, we're coming out tonight,
To dance by the light of the moon.

I danced with a gal with a hole in her stocking,
And her heel kept a rockin' and her toe kept a-knockin'.
I danced with a gal with a hole in her stocking
And we danced by the light of the moon.

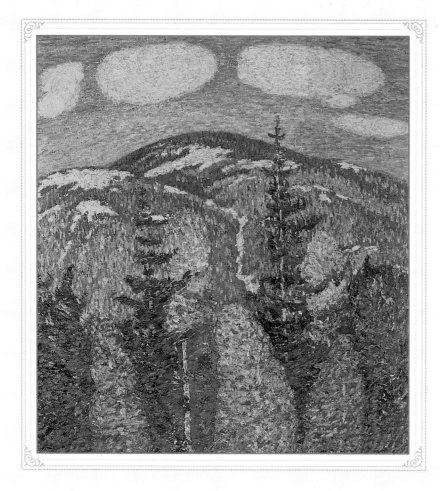

America the Beautiful

BY KATHARINE LEE BATES AND SAMUEL A. WARD (1893)

American poet Katherine Lee Bates wrote the words to this beloved anthem after an inspiring visit to the summit of Pike's Peak.

O beautiful for spacious skies,

For amber waves of grain,

For purple mountain majesties

Above the fruited plain.

America! America!

God shed his grace on thee,

And crown thy good with brotherhood

From sea to shining sea.

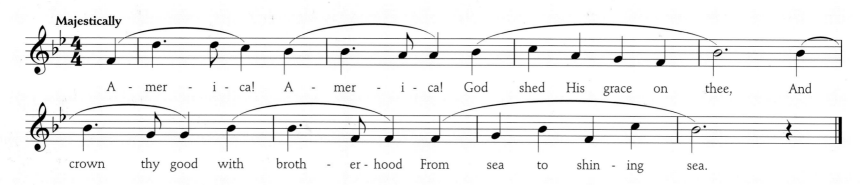

Moon Over Miami

BY EDGAR LESLIE AND JOE BURKE (1935)

This song title has inspired some of the greatest sheet-music
art ever printed.

Moon over Miami, shine on my love and me,
So we can stroll beside the roll of the rolling sea.
Moon over Miami, shine on as we begin,
A dream or two that may come true when the tide comes in.

Hark to the song of the smiling troubadours,
Hark to the throbbing guitars.
Hear how the waves offer thunderous applause
After each song to the stars.
Moon over Miami, you know we're waiting for
A little love, a little kiss on Miami shore.

Moon o-ver Mi-a-mi, shine on my love and
me, So we can stroll be-side the
roll of the roll-ing sea.

California, Here I Come

by Al Jolson, Bud DeSylva, and Joseph Meyer (1924)

This show-stopping tune was written for the electric presence and inimitable voice of one of Broadway's biggest attractions—Al Jolson.

California, here I come, right back where I started from.
Where bowers of flowers bloom in the sun,
Each morning at dawning, birdies sing and everything.
A sunkist miss said, "Don't be late," that's why
    I can hardly wait.
Open up that Golden Gate, California, here I come.

The Ballad of Davy Crockett

BY TOM BLACKBURN AND GEORGE BRUNS (1954)

*This is the theme song from the popular Walt Disney
television series* The Adventures of Davy Crockett.

Born on a mountaintop in Tennessee,

Greenest state in the land of the free,

Raised in the woods so's he knew every tree,

Kilt him a b'ar when he was only three.

Davy, Davy Crockett, king of the wild frontier.

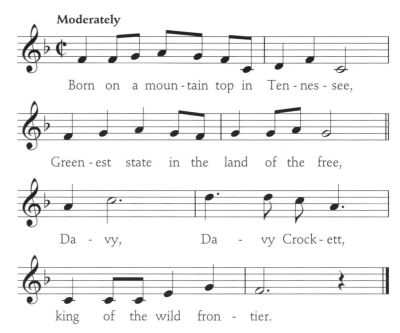

Born on a moun-tain top in Ten-nes-see,

Green-est state in the land of the free,

Da-vy, Da-vy Crock-ett,

king of the wild fron-tier.

Red River Valley

BY JAMES KERRIGAN (1890)

The musical film King of the Cowboys, *starring Roy Rogers and Smiley Burnette, pays tribute to this traditional cowboy favorite.*

From this valley they say you are going;
We will miss your bright eyes and sweet smile,
For they say you are taking the sunshine
That has brightened our pathway a while.

Come and sit by my side if you love me.
Do not hasten to bid me adieu,
But remember the Red River Valley
And the cowboy that loves you so true.

Won't you think of this valley you're leaving?
Oh, how lonely, how sad it will be.
Oh, think of the fond heart you're breaking
And the grief you are causing me.

As you go to your home by the ocean
May you never forget those sweet hours
That we spent in the Red River Valley
And the love we exchanged 'mid the flowers.

But re-mem-ber the Red Ri-ver Val-ley_____ And the cow-boy that loves you so true._____

Git Along Little Dogies

AUTHOR UNKNOWN (1870s)

*The melody of this cowboy song is vaguely Irish, but "Whoopee ti yi yo" is strictly American:
a sharp rhythmic cry to energize sluggish cattle without frightening them. Dogies is a
term cowboys used to refer to cattle.*

As I walked out one morning for
   pleasure,
I spied a cowpuncher a-ridin' alone;
His hat was thrown back and his spurs
   were a-jinglin'
As he approached me a-singin' this song:

Whoopee ti yi yo, git along little dogies.
It's your misfortune and none of my own.
Whoopie to yi yo, git along little dogies.
For you know Wyoming will be your
   new home.

Early in the spring we round up the dogies,
Mark 'em and brand 'em and bob off
   their tails;

Round up our horses, load up the
   chuckwagon,
Then throw the dogies upon the old trail.

It's whooping and yelling and driving
   the dogies;
Oh, how I wish you would go on!
It's whooping and punching and go on
   little dogies,
For you know Wyoming will be your
   new home.

Whoopee ti yi yo, git along little dogies.
It's your misfortune and none of my own.

Loping

Whoop-ee ti yi yo, git a-long lit-tle do-gies, For you know Wy-om-ing will be your new home.

On Top of Old Smoky

AUTHOR UNKNOWN (1840s)

*Sometimes in the Blue Ridge Mountains the fog gets so thick that
the mountains seem made of smoke. No one knows who wrote this
ballad, but its wistful admission of loneliness made it popular in
the pioneer days.*

On top of Old Smoky, all covered with snow,
I lost my true lover, by courting too slow.

Well, courting's a pleasure, and parting a grief
But a false-hearted lover is worse than a thief.

A thief, he will rob you and take all you have,
But a false-hearted lover will send you to your grave.

They'll hug you and kiss you and tell you more lies
Than the cross ties on the railroad or the stars in the skies.

They'll tell you they love you just to give your heart ease,
And just as soon as your back's turned, they'll court whom
    they please.

I'll go back to Old Smoky, Old Smoky so high,
Where the wild birds and turtledoves can hear my sad cry.

On top of Old Smo - ky,_____ all cov - ered with snow,

The Yellow Rose of Texas

AUTHOR UNKNOWN (1858)

Also known as "The Song of the Texas Rangers."

There's a Yellow Rose of Texas I'm goin' for to see,
No other soldier knows her, nobody, only me.
She cried so when I left her, it like to broke my heart,
And if I ever find her, we nevermore will part.

She's the sweetest rose of color this soldier ever knew.
Her eyes are bright as diamonds, they sparkle like the dew.
You may talk about your winsome maids and sing of Rosalie,
But the Yellow Rose of Texas beats the belles of Tennessee.

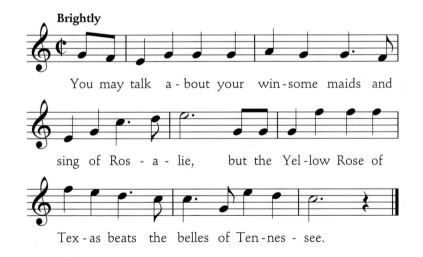

Brightly

You may talk a-bout your win-some maids and

sing of Ros-a-lie,   but the Yel-low Rose of

Tex-as beats the belles of Ten-nes-see.

Skip to My Lou

AUTHOR UNKNOWN (1880s)

Young people in most 19th-century rural towns were barred from dancing for religious reasons. Dancing was considered sinful—but playing games wasn't. As a result, "play party games" accompanied by clapping and singing, such as this one, evolved.

Lost my partner, what'll I do?
Lost my partner, what'll I do?
Lost my partner, what'll I do?
Skip to my lou, my darling.

Skip, skip, skip to my lou
Skip, skip, skip to my lou
Skip, skip, skip to my lou
Skip to my lou, my darling.

I'll get another one prettier than you
I'll get another one prettier than you
I'll get another one prettier than you
Skip to my lou, my darling.

Skip, skip, skip to my lou
Skip, skip, skip to my lou
Skip, skip, skip to my lou
Skip to my lou, my darling.

Flies in the buttermilk, shoo, fly, shoo!
Flies in the buttermilk, shoo, fly, shoo!
Flies in the buttermilk, shoo, fly, shoo!
Skip to my lou, my darling.

Skip, skip, skip to my lou
Skip, skip, skip to my lou
Skip, skip, skip to my lou
Skip to my lou, my darling.

Brightly

Skip,— skip,— skip to my lou Skip,— skip,— skip to my lou,

Skip,— skip,— skip to my lou Skip to my lou, my dar - ling.

Take Me out to the Ball Game

BY JACK NORWORTH AND ALBERT VON TILZER (1908)

Jack Norworth, a vaudeville actor, wrote the words. Albert von Tilzer wrote the music—some twenty years before he actually saw his first baseball game.

Take me out to the ball game,

Take me out to the crowd.

Buy me some peanuts and Cracker Jack,

I don't care if I never come back.

And it's root, root, root for the home team,

If they don't win it's a shame.

For it's one, two, three strikes, "You're out!"

At the old ball game.

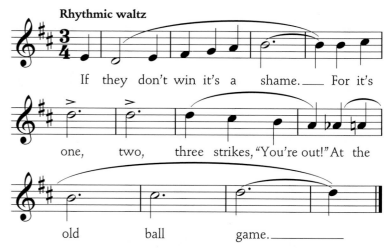

Clementine

BY PERCY MONTROSS (1880s)

Women were scarce in the California gold-mining camps, so you'd think songs about woman would be pleasant and romantic. Not so with the unfortunate Clementine. Today singers of all ages make up their own versions—like "Found a Peanut."

In a cavern, in a canyon, excavating for a mine,
Lived a miner, forty-niner, and his daughter Clemetine.
Oh, my darling, oh, my darling, oh, my darling Clementine!
You are lost and gone forever, dreadful sorry, Clementine.

Light she was and like a fairy, and her shoes were number nine.
Herring boxes without topses, sandals were for Clementine.
Oh, my darling, oh, my darling, oh, my darling Clementine!
You are lost and gone forever, dreadful sorry, Clementine.

Drove her ducklings to the water, every morning just at nine.
Hit her foot against a splinter, fell into the foaming brine.
Oh, my darling, oh, my darling, oh, my darling Clementine!
You are lost and gone forever, dreadful sorry, Clementine.

Ruby lips above the water, blowing bubbles soft and fine.
But, alas, I was no swimmer, so I lost my Clementine.
Oh, my darling, oh, my darling, oh, my darling Clementine!
You are lost and gone forever, dreadful sorry, Clementine.

How I missed her, how I missed her, how I missed my Clementine,
Till I kissed her little sister, and forgot my Clementine.

Yankee Doodle

BY RICHARD SHACKBURG (1758)

During the Revolution, this tune was also known as the
"Lexington March" and could be heard at many important battle
sites, including Bunker Hill and Lexington.

Yankee Doodle went to town,
A-riding on a pony;
Stuck a feather in his cap,
And called it macaroni.

Yankee Doodle keep it up,
Yankee Doodle dandy,
Mind the music and the step,
And with the girls be handy.

Father and I went down to camp,
Along with Captain Gooding;
And there we saw the men and boys,
As thick as hasty pudding.

God Bless America

BY IRVING BERLIN (1938)

Irving Berlin's tribute to America was performed most memorably on radio broadcasts during World War II by the remarkable Kate Smith.

Oh, God bless America,

Land that I love,

Stand beside Her,

And guide Her,

Through the night

With the light from above.

From the mountains,

To the prairies,

To the oceans,

White with foam,

God bless America,

My home sweet home.

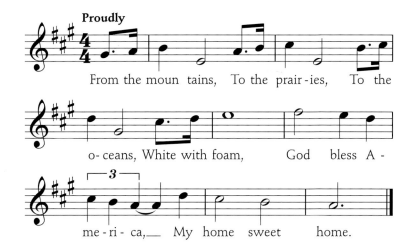

Row, Row, Row Your Boat

Author unknown (1852)

Paul McCartney of the Beatles proclaimed this the greatest song of all time.

Row, row, row your boat,
Gently down the stream,
Merrily, merrily, merrily, merrily,
Life is but a dream.

Row, row, row your boat,
Sweetly as you go,
Lovelier, lovelier, lovelier, lovelier,
Joy is all you know.

The Sidewalks of New York

BY JAMES BLAKE AND CHARLES LAWLOR (1894)

This rousing song, also known as "East Side, West Side," has been the favorite theme song of New York City for more than a century.

Down in front of Casey's old brown wooden stoop
On a summer's evening we formed a merry group.
Boys and girls together, we would sing and waltz
While Tony played the organ on the sidewalks of New York.

Eastside, westside, all around the town
The gang played ring-a-rosy, London Bridge is falling down.
Boys and girls together, me and Mamie O'Rourke
We'd trip the light fantastic on the sidewalks of New York.

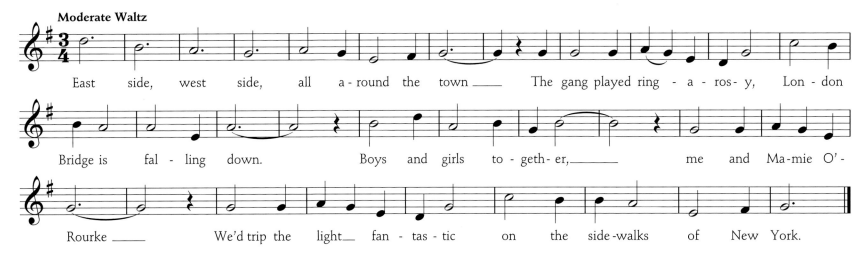

Moderate Waltz

East side, west side, all a-round the town —— The gang played ring - a - ros - y, Lon - don
Bridge is fal - ling down. Boys and girls to - geth - er,———— me and Ma-mie O'-
Rourke —— We'd trip the light— fan - tas - tic on the side-walks of New York.

Summertime

BY DUBOSE HEYWARD AND GEORGE GERSHWIN (1935)

From Gershwin's highly acclaimed musical Porgy and Bess.

Summertime and the livin' is easy,
Fish are jumpin' and the cotton is high.
Oh, your pappa's rich and your momma's good lookin',
So hush, little baby, don't you cry.

One of these mornings you're goin' rise up singin'
Then you'll spread your wings and you'll take for the sky.
Until that mornin' there ain't nothin' can harm you
With momma and pappa standin' by.

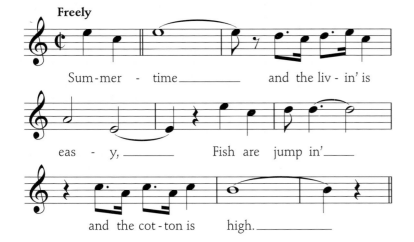

Camptown Races

BY STEPHEN FOSTER (1850)

Often entitled "Doo Dah" or "Goin' to Run All Night," this brilliant song was written by the great and prolific songwriter Stephen Foster and popularized by the original Christy Minstrels.

O the Camptown ladies sing this song, doodah, doodah.
The Camptown race track's five miles long, oh doodah day.
Goin' to run all night, goin' to run all day,
I bet my money on a bob-tailed nag, somebody bet on the bay.

I went down south with my hat caved in, doodah, doodah.
I came back north with a pocket full of tin, oh doodah day.
Goin' to run all night, goin' to run all day,
I bet my money on a bob-tailed nag, somebody bet on the bay.

You're a Grand Old Flag

by George M. Cohan (1906)

The song was first introduced in the 1906 musical George Washington Jr. *by George M. Cohan, who also appeared in the production.*

You're a grand old flag, you're a high-flying flag;
And forever in peace may you wave;
You're the emblem of the land I love,
The home of the free and brave.
Every heart beats true 'neath the Red, White, and Blue,
Where there's never a boast or brag;
But should auld acquaintance be forgot,
Keep your eye on the grand old flag.

With Spirit

You're a grand old flag, you're a
high fly-ing flag; And for-ev-er in
peace may you wave;

Battle Hymn of the Republic

BY JULIA WARD HOWE (1862)

*It is said that a dream inspired Julia Ward Howe to write these famous lyrics,
and she completed the verses just a few hours after waking.*

Mine eyes have seen the glory of the coming of the Lord;

He is trampling out the vintage where the grapes of wrath are stored;

He hath loos'd the fateful lighting of his terrible swift sword,

His truth is marching on.

Glory, glory, hallelujah! Glory, glory, hallelujah!

Glory, glory, hallelujah! His truth is marching on.

I have seen Him in the watch-fires of a hundred circling camps;

They have builded Him an altar in the evening dews and damps;

I can read His righteous sentence by the dim and flaring lamps,

His day is marching on.

In the beauty of the lilies Christ was born across the sea,

With a glory in His bosom that transfigures you and me;

As He died to make men holy, let us die to make men free,

While God is marching on.

Sweet Betsy From Pike

AUTHOR UNKNOWN (1853)

This song commemorates the rugged life of the Western pioneer with an amusing portrait of two hearty forty-niners journeying by wagon from Missouri to California.

Oh, don't you remember Sweet Betsy from Pike?
Who crossed the big mountains with her lover Ike.
With two yoke of oxen, a big yaller dog,
A tall Shanghai rooster, and one spotted hog.

One evening quite early they camped on the Platte,
'Twas near by the road on a green shady flat.
Where Betsy, sore-footed, lay down to repose,
With wonder I gazed on his Pike County rose.

The Shanghai ran off, and their cattle all died,
That morning the last piece of bacon was fried.
Poor Ike was discouraged and Betsy got mad.
The dog dropped his tail and looked wondrously sad.

They soon reached the desert, where Betsy gave out,
And down in the sand she lay rolling about.
While Ike, half distracted, looked on with surprise,
Saying, "Betsy, get up, you'll get sand in your eyes."

Sweet Betsy got up in a great deal of pain,
Declared she'd go back to Pike County again;
But Ike gave a sigh, and they fondly embraced,
And they travel along with his arm round her waist.

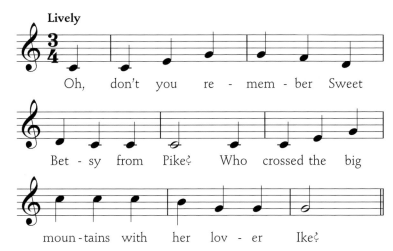

Tennessee Waltz

BY REDD STEWART AND PEE WEE KING (1948)

*Patti Page's 1950 recording of this song set two records at the time:
it stayed on the Billboard charts for more than two years and was
number one for nearly nine months.*

I was dancin' with my darlin' to the Tennessee waltz
When an old friend I happened to see.
Introduced him to my loved one and while they
    were waltzing
My friend stole my sweetheart from me.

I remember the night and the Tennessee waltz.
Now I know just how much I have lost.
Yes, I lost my little darlin' the night they were playing
The beautiful Tennessee Waltz.

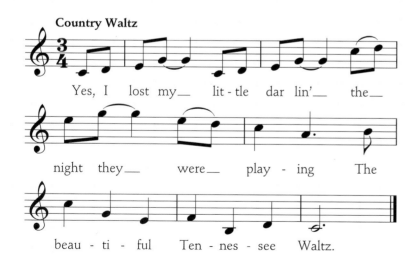

Country Waltz

Yes, I lost my__ lit-tle dar lin'__ the__
night they__ were__ play - ing The
beau - ti - ful Ten - nes - see Waltz.

Jeanie with the Light Brown Hair

BY STEPHEN FOSTER (1850s)

Considered by The Grand Ole Oprey *to be the first*
"country music ballad."

I dream of Jeanie with the light brown hair,

Borne like a zephyr on the summer air,

I happy as the daisies that dance on her way.

Many were the wild notes her merry voice would pour,

Many were the blithe birds that warbled them o'er,

Oh, floating like a vapor on the soft summer air.

I see her tripping where the bright streams play,

I dream of Jeanie with the light brown hair.

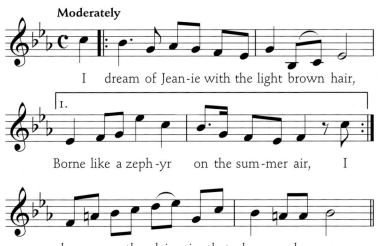

Moderately

I dream of Jean-ie with the light brown hair,

Borne like a zeph-yr on the sum-mer air, I

hap-py as the dais - ies that dance on her way.

She'll Be Coming Round the Mountain

AUTHOR UNKNOWN (1900)

This well-known dance and sing-along song was a favorite with railroad workers, who added many alternate verses.

She'll be coming round the mountain when she comes,
She'll be coming round the mountain when she comes,
She'll be coming round the mountain
She'll be coming round the mountain
She'll be coming round the mountain when she comes.

She'll be driving six white horses when she comes,
She'll be driving six white horses when she comes,
She'll be driving six white horses
She'll be driving six white horses
She'll be driving six white horses when she comes.

Oh, we'll all go down to meet her when she comes,
Oh, we'll all go down to meet her when she comes,
Oh, we'll all go down to meet her
Oh, we'll all go down to meet her
Oh, we'll all go down to meet her when she comes.

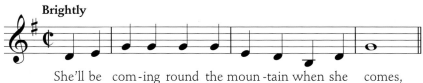

Carolina in the Morning

BY GUS KAHN AND WALTER DONALDSON (1922)

This vaudeville crooning classic most famously sung by Bing Crosby was one of comedian George Burns's favorites.

Nothing could be finer than to be in Carolina in the morning,

No one could be sweeter than my sweetheart when I meet her in the morning,

Strolling with my girlie where the dew is pearlie early in the morning,

Butterflies all flutter up and kiss each little buttercup at dawn.

Where the morning glories twine around the door,

Whispering pretty stories I long to hear once more.

If I had Aladdin's lamp for only one day,

I'd make a wish and here's what I'd say,

Nothing could be finer than to be in Carolina in the morning.

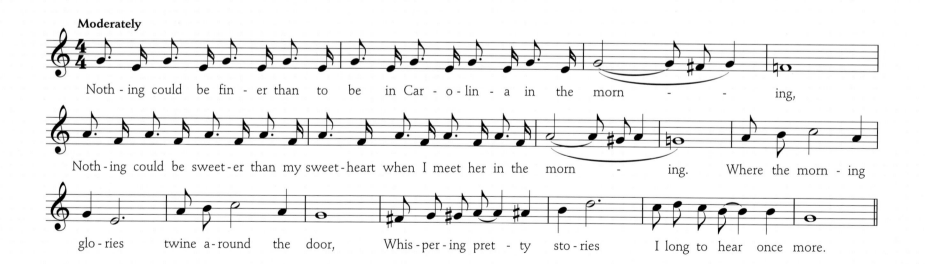

Nothing could be finer than to be in Carolina in the morning,

Nothing could be sweeter than my sweetheart when I meet her in the morning. Where the morning

glories twine around the door, Whispering pretty stories I long to hear once more.

Polly Wolly Doodle

Author unknown (Late 1800s)

A traditional Southern fiddle classic.

Oh, I went down South for to see my Sal,

Singing Polly Wolly Doodle all the day.

My Sally is a spunky gal,

Singing Polly Wolly Doodle all the day.

Oh, my Sal, she is a maiden fair

Singing Polly Wolly Doodle all the day.

With curly eyes and laughing hair

Singing Polly Wolly Doodle all the day.

Fare thee well, fare thee well,

Fare thee well, my fairy fay,

For I'm going to Lousiana,

For to see my Susyanna,

Singing Polly Wolly Doodle all the day.

Sing-ing Pol-ly Wol-ly Doo-dle all the day.

Meet Me in St. Louis, Louis

BY ANDREW B. STERLING AND KERRY MILLS (1904)

Written to commemorate the St. Louis Exposition of 1904,
this became the title song for a 1944 musical film starring
Judy Garland.

Meet me in St. Louis, Louis, meet me at the fair,
Don't tell me the lights are shining any place but there,
We will dance the Hoochee Koochee,
I will be your tootsie wootsie;
Meet me in St. Louis, Louis, meet me at the fair.

Moderately

Meet me in St. Lou - is, Lou - is, meet me at the fair,_____

Don't tell me the lights are shin - ing an - y place but there._____

Blow the Man Down

Author unknown (1860)

Like other sea shanties, this song's pulsing, regular beat helped crews maintain a concerted effort while hoisting the sails, weighing the anchor, or performing other shipboard tasks.

Come all you young fellows that follow
    the sea,
With a way, hey, blow the man down,
Now please pay attention and listen to me,
Give me some time to blow the man down.

There are tinkers and tailors, shoemakers
    and all,
With a way, hey, blow the man down,
They're all shipped for sailors on board the
    Black Ball,
Give me some time to blow the man down.

As I was a-walking down Paradise Street
With a way, hey, blow the man down,
A pretty damsel I chanced for to meet,
Give me some time to blow the man down.

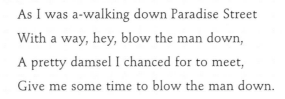

With a lilt

Come all ye young fel-lows that fol-low the sea, With a way, hey, blow the man down, Give me some time to blow the man down.

Ol' Man River

BY OSCAR HAMMERSTEIN AND JEROME KERN (1927)

From the hit musical Showboat, *this song was first performed by the legendary Paul Robeson.*

Ol' man river, dat ol' man river,

He must know sumpin', but don't say nothin'

He jus' keeps rollin', He just keeps on rollin' along.

He don't plant 'taters, he don't plant cotton,

An' dem dat plants 'em is soon forgotten,

But ol' man river, he just keeps rollin' along.

I've Been Working on the Railroad

AUTHOR UNKNOWN (1870S)

Dinah was perhaps a train or a real woman, with "blow your horn" meaning "call me for lunch." "Someone's in the kitchen with Dinah" was actually a separate song, but because of the "Dinah" connection, it came to be linked with this one.

I've been working on the railroad,

All the live long day,

I've been working on the railroad,

Just to pass the time away.

Don't you hear the whistle blowing?

Rise up so early in the morn,

Don't you hear the captain shouting,

"Dinah, blow your horn!

Dinah, won't you blow,

Dinah won't you blow,

Dinah, won't you blow your horn!"

Someone's in the kitchen with Dinah,

Someone's in the kitchen, I know.

Someone's in the kitchen with Dinah,

Strumming on the old banjo and singing:

Fee fi fiddlee-i-o, fee fi fiddlee-i-o,

Fee fi fiddlee-i-o,

Strumming on the old banjo.

Vigorously

I've been work-ing on the rail - road,

All the live long day.

Back Home Again in Indiana

BY BALLARD MCDONALD AND JAMES F. HANLEY (1917)

The official state song of Indiana, this is played each year before the famous Indianapolis 500 car race.

Back home again in Indiana,
And it seems that I can see
The gleaming candlelight still shining bright
Through the sycamore for me.

The new-mown hay sends all its fragrance
From the fields I used to roam,
When I dream about the moonlight on the Wabash
Then I long for my Indiana's home.

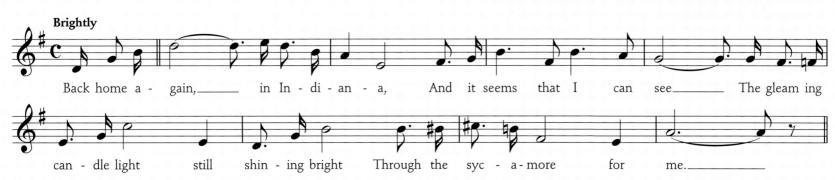

Back in the Saddle Again

BY GENE AUTRY (1941)

*Singing cowboy movie star Gene Autry wrote this, and it became
the theme song for his 1950s TV series,* The Gene Autry Show,
which costarred his horse Champion.

Whoopie ti yi oh! Rockin' to 'n' fro
Back in the saddle again
Whoopie ti yi ay! I go my way
I'm back in the saddle again.

I'm back in the saddle again
Out where a friend is a friend
Where the long-horned cattle feed
On the lowly jimsonweed
I'm back in the saddle again.

I'm out on the range once more
Totin' my old forty-four.
I sleep out every night
Where the only law is right
I'm back in the saddle again.

Moderately

I'm back in the sad-dle a - gain,_____ out where a friend is a friend.

Turkey in the Straw

AUTHOR UNKNOWN (1834)

*This traditional fiddle tune has become the mainstay of the
American square dance.*

As I was a going down the road

With a tired team and a heavy load,

I cracked my whip and the leader sprung;

I says, "Day day" to the wagon tongue.

Turkey in the straw, haw, haw, haw,

Turkey in the hay, hay, hay, hay,

Roll 'em up and twist 'em up a high tuck-a-haw,

And hit 'em up a tune called "Turkey in the Straw!"

Oh, I went out to milk and I didn't know how.

I milked the goat instead of the cow.

A monkey sitting on a pile of straw

A-winking his eye at his mother-in-law.

Turkey in the straw, haw, haw, haw,

Turkey in the hay, hay, hay, hay,

Roll 'em up and twist 'em up a high tuck-a-haw,

And hit 'em up a tune called "Turkey in the Straw!"

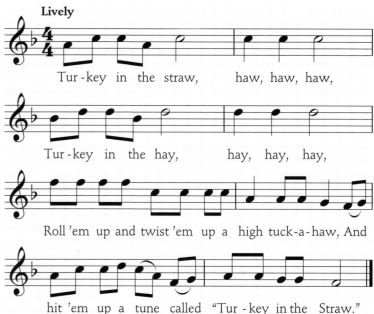

The Mockingbird Song

AUTHOR UNKNOWN (1840s)

Popular in the South during pioneer days, this song descends from an old English nursery rhyme. Now it's possibly the best-known lullaby in America.

Hush, little baby, don't say a word.
Papa's gonna buy you a mockingbird.
And if that mockingbird won't sing,
Papa's gonna buy you a diamond ring.

And if that diamond ring is brass,
Papa's gonna buy you a looking glass.
And if that looking glass gets broke,
Papa's gonna buy you a billy goat.

And if that billy goat won't pull,
Papa's gonna buy you a cart and bull.
And if that cart and bull fall down,
You'll still be the sweetest little baby in town.

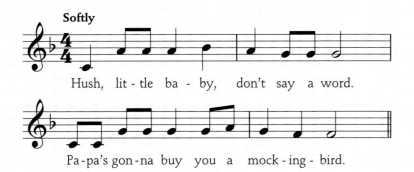

Hush, lit-tle ba-by, don't say a word.

Pa-pa's gon-na buy you a mock-ing-bird.

Swannee River

BY STEPHEN FOSTER (1851)

Stephen Foster sold this song for fifteen dollars to E. P. Christy of the Christy Minstrels. The overwhelming success of this classic minstrel song established Foster as America's most important songwriter and in the early 1900s made Al Jolson America's greatest entertainer of the time.

'Way down upon the Swannee River, far, far away,
There's where my heart is turning ever,
There's where the old folks stay.
All up and down the whole creation, sadly I roam,
Still longing for the old plantation
And for the old folks at home.

All the world is sad and dreary, everywhere I roam
O brothers, how my heart grows weary
Far from the old folks at home.

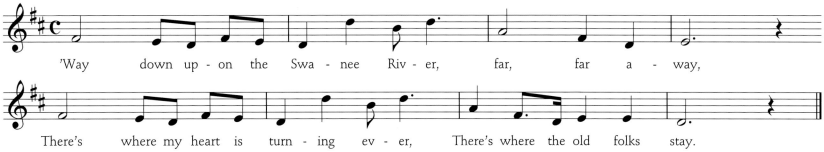

'Way down up-on the Swa-nee Riv-er, far, far a-way,
There's where my heart is turn-ing ev-er, There's where the old folks stay.

The Star Spangled Banner

BY FRANCIS SCOTT KEY AND JOHN STAFFORD SMITH (1778)

*The words to our national anthem were written during the
Revolutionary War, when the author saw the American flag waving
atop Fort McHenry after a night of relentless bombardment from
enemy ships.*

Oh, say, can you see, by the dawn's early light,

What so proudly we hailed at the twilight's last gleaming?

Whose broad stripes and bright stars, through the
    perilous fight,

O'er the ramparts we watched were so gallantly streaming?

And the rocket's red glare, the bombs bursting in air,

Gave proof through the night that our flag was still there.

Oh, say, does that star spangled banner yet wave,

O'er the land of the free and the home of the brave?

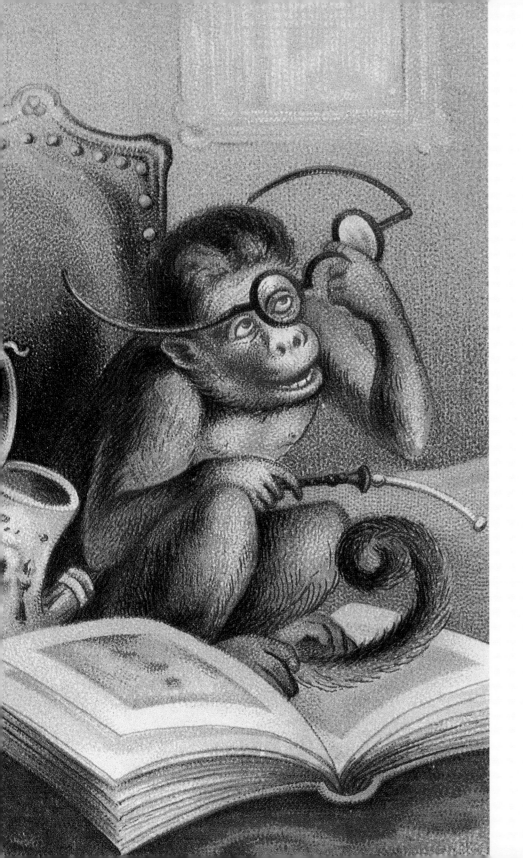

Pop Goes the Weasel

Author unknown (Late 1800s)

A childlike square-dance favorite throughout Texas, Louisiana, and Arkansas.

All around the cobbler's bench,
The monkey chased the weasel;
The monkey thought 'twas all in fun.
Pop goes the weasel!

Rather quickly

All a-round the cob-bler's bench, The
mon-key chased the wea-sel; The
mon-key thought 'twas all in fun.
Pop goes the wea-sel!

Over the River and Through the Wood

BY LYDIA MARIA CHILD (1900)

When the third and fourth stanzas were added some sixty years ago, this song became a Thanksgiving favorite.

Over the river and through the wood,
To grandfather's house we go,
The horse knows the way
To carry the sleigh
Through the white and drifted snow.

Over the river and through the wood,
Oh how the wind does blow!
It stings the toes,
And bites the nose,
As over the ground we go.

Over the river and through the wood,
To have a first-rate play.
Hear the bells ring,
Ting-a-ling-ding!
Hurrah for Thanksgiving Day!

Over the river and through the wood.
Trot fast, my dapple gray!
Spring over the ground,
Like a hunting hound!
For this is Thanksgiving Day.

Over the river and through the wood,
And straight through the barnyard gate.
We seem to go
Extremely slow,
It is so hard to wait!

Over the river and through the wood,
Now grandmother's cap I spy!
Hurrah for the fun!
Is the pudding done?
Hurrah for the pumpkin pie!

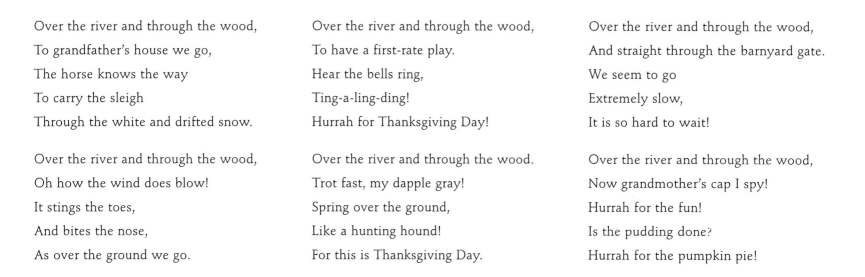

Amazing Grace

BY JOHN NEWTON (EARLY 1800S)

The words to this inspiring hymn were penned by the Reverend John Newton, a slave-ship captain who underwent a spiritual awakening and began a new life in the ministry.

Amazing grace! How sweet
　　the sound
That saved a soul like me
I once was lost and now
　　am found
Was blind but now can see.

'Twas grace that taught my
　　heart to fear
And grace my fears relieved
How precious did that grace
　　appear
The hour I first believed.

The Lord has promised good to me
His word my hope secures
He will my shield and portion be
As long as life endures.

Through many dangers, toils,
　　and snares
I have already come
'Tis grace that brought me safe
　　thus far
And grace will lead me home.

When we've been there ten
　　thousand years
Bright shining as the sun
We've no less days to sing
　　God's praise
Than when we first begun.

Amazing grace has set me free
To touch, to taste, to feel
The wonders of accepting love
Have made me whole and real.

A - maz - ing___ grace! How sweet the sound

'Tis a Gift to Be Simple

AUTHOR UNKNOWN (1848)

*The early Shakers used to dance and "shake" to melodies
like this one.*

'Tis a gift to be simple, 'tis a gift to be free,

'Tis a gift to come down to where we ought to be.

And when we find ourselves in the place just right,

'Twill be in the valley of love and delight.

When true simplicity is gained,

To bow and bend we won't be ashamed.

To turn, turn, will be our delight,

Till by turning and turning we come around right.

'Tis a gift to be sim-ple, 'tis a gift to be free, 'Tis a gift to come down to where we ought to be.

The Wabash Cannonball

AUTHOR UNKNOWN (CIRCA 1860S)

Signature tune of Dizzy Dean, Baseball Hall of Famer and TV announcer,

who sang it during each seventh-inning stretch.

From the great Atlantic Ocean to the wide Pacific shore,

From the queen of flowing rivers, through the southland's verdant door.

She's mighty tall and handsome, and known quite well by all;

She's the reg'lar combination of the Wabash Cannonball.

Well, listen to the jingle, the rumble, and the roar,

As she glides along the woodland, through the hills and the shore.

Hear the mighty rush of the engine, and the lonesome whistle's call;

She's the reg'lar combination of the Wabash Cannonball.

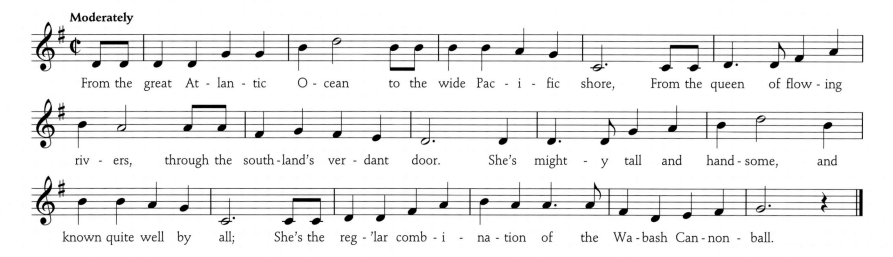

Georgia on My Mind

BY STUART GORRELL AND HOAGY CARMICHAEL (1930)

*Carmichael's composition became a big hit for Ray Charles
in the 1960s.*

Georgia, Georgia, the whole day through.

Just an old sweet song keeps Georgia on my mind.

Georgia, Georgia, a song of you

Comes as sweet and clear as moonlight through the pines.

Other arms reach out to me, other eyes smile tenderly,

Still in peaceful dreams I see the road leads back to you.

Georgia, Georgia, no peace I find,

Just an old, sweet song keeps Georgia on my mind.

Big Rock Candy Mountain

BY HARRY McCLINTOCK (LATE 1800S)

This hobo anthem was featured in the 1949 film Nighttime
in Nevada, *starring Roy Rogers and Andy Devine.*

One evening as the sun went down
And the jungle fires were burning
Down the track came a hobo hiking
He said "Boys, I'm not turning,
I'm heading for a land that's far away
Beside that crystal fountain.
I'll see you all this coming fall
On the Big Rock Candy Mountain."

On the Big Rock Candy Mountain
It's a land that's fair and bright.
The handouts grow on bushes
And you sleep out ev'ry night.
The boxcars are all empty
And the sun shines every day.
I'm bound to go where there ain't no snow
Where the sleet don't fall and the winds don't blow
On the Big Rock Candy Mountain.

Oh, the buzzing of the bees in the cigarette trees
By the soda water fountain
Near the lemonade springs where the bluebird sings
On the Big Rock Candy Mountain.

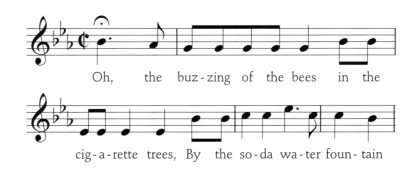

Happy Days Are Here Again

BY JACK YELLEN AND MILTON AGER (1929)

Franklin D. Roosevelt and his Democratic Party made this their theme song during their successful campaign for president of the United States in the 1930s.

Happy days are here again!
The skies above are clear again.
Let us sing a song of cheer again,
Happy days are here again!

Your cares and troubles are gone;
There'll be no more from now on.
All together shout it now!
There's no one who can doubt it now,
So let's tell the world about it now,
Happy days are here again!

Hap - py days__ are here a - gain!__ The skies a - bove__ are clear a - gain.__ Let us sing a song__ of cheer a - gain, __ Hap - py days are here a - gain!__

Tea for Two

BY RHODA ROBERTS, KENNY JACOBSON, AND
MOE KOFFMAN (1924)

This song debuted in the Broadway musical No, No, Nanette.

Picture you upon my knee

Just tea for two and two for tea

Just me for you and you for me alone

Nobody near us to see us or hear us

No friends or relations on weekend vacations

We won't have it known, dear, that we own a telephone, dear.

Day will break and you'll awake

And start to bake a sugar cake

For me to take for all the boys to see

We will raise a family—a boy for you, a girl for me

Oh can't you see how happy we would be?

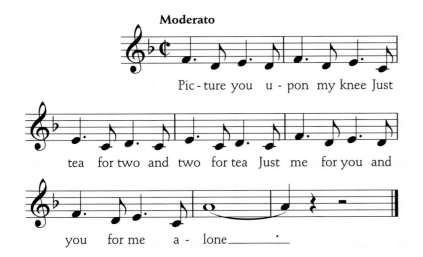

The Stars and Stripes Forever

BY JOHN PHILIP SOUSA (1897)

The most recognized downbeat in the history of music.

Challenged only by the theme song to the movie 2001 by Stanley Kubrick.

Let martial note in triumph float
And liberty extend its mighty hand
A flag appears 'mid thunderous cheers,
The banner of the Western land.
The emblem of the brave and true
Its folds protect no tyrant crew;
The red and white and starry blue
Is freedom's shield and hope.
Other nations may deem their flag's the best

And cheer them with fervid elation
But the flag of the North and South
    and West
Is the flag of flags, the flag of
    Freedom's nation.

Hurrah for the flag of the free!
May it wave as our standard forever,
The gem of the land and the sea,

The banner of the right.
Let despots remember the day
When our fathers with mighty endeavor
Proclaimed as they marched to the fray
That by their might and by their right
It waves forever.

Brightly

Hur - rah for the flag of the free!___ May it wave as our stan-dard for-e - ver, The

gem of the land and the sea,___ The ban-ner of the right.___ Let des-pots re-

mem-ber the day___ When our fath-ers with migh-ty en-dea - vor Pro - claimed as they

marched to the fray___ That by their might and by their right It waves for-e - ver.

Home on the Range

by Brewster Higley and Dan Kelly (1873)

This song, first titled "My Western Home," originally did not include the words "home on the range." But it mutated into "the cowboys' national anthem," becoming the favorite song of Franklin D. Roosevelt.

Oh, give me a home where the buffalo roam,
Where the deer and the antelope play,
Where seldom is heard a discouraging word,
And the skies are not cloudy all day.

How often at night when the heavens are bright
With the light from the glittering stars,
Have I stood here amazed and asked as I gazed
If their glory exceeds that of ours.

Home, home on the range,
Where the deer and the antelope play,
Where seldom is heard a discouraging word,
And the skies are not cloudy all day.

The Man on the Flying Trapeze

by Walter O'Keefe (1860s)

Sung by the singing clowns in small circuses before the Civil War.

Once I was happy but now I'm forlorn

Like an old coat that is tatter'd and torn

I'm left in this wide world to fret and to mourn

Betray'd by a maid in her teens

Now the girl that I lov'd, she was handsome

And I tried all I knew, her to please

But I never could please her a quarter as well

As the man on the flying trapeze! Whoa!

He flies through the air with the greatest of ease

This daring young man on the flying trapeze

His movements are graceful, all girls he does please

And my love he's stolen away.

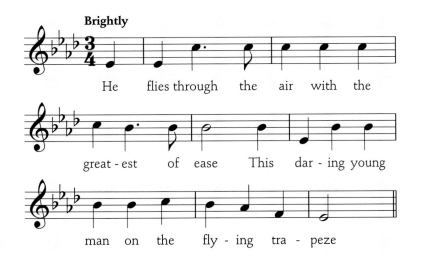

Brightly

He flies through the air with the

great - est of ease This dar - ing young

man on the fly - ing tra - peze

This Land Is Your Land

BY WOODY GUTHRIE (1940)

Folksinger Woody Guthrie's "love song to America" has become an honorary national anthem.

This land is your land, this land is my land,
From California to the New York Island,
From the redwood forest to the gulfstream
    waters,
This land was made for you and me.

As I went walking that ribbon of highway
I saw above me that endless skyway,
I saw below me that golden valley—
This land was made for you and me.

As I went rambling that dusty highway
I saw a sign that said, "Private Property,"
But on the other side it didn't say nothing—
That side was made for you and me.

Nobody living can ever stop me
As I go walking my freedom highway.
Nobody living can make me turn back—
This land was made for you and me.

This land is your land, this land is my land,
From California to the New York Island,
From the redwood forest to the gulfstream
    waters,
This land was made for you and me.

Happy Trails

BY DALE EVANS (1951)

*Dale Evans's slow, tender words and music concluded every broadcast of
her husband's television series,* The Roy Rogers Show.

Some trails are happy ones,
Others are blue.
It's the way you ride the trail that counts;
Here's a happy one for you.

Happy trails to you until we meet again
Happy trails to you, keep smilin' until then.

Who cares about the clouds
When we're together?
Just sing a song
And bring the sunny weather.

Happy trails to you until we meet again
Happy trails to you, keep smilin' until then.

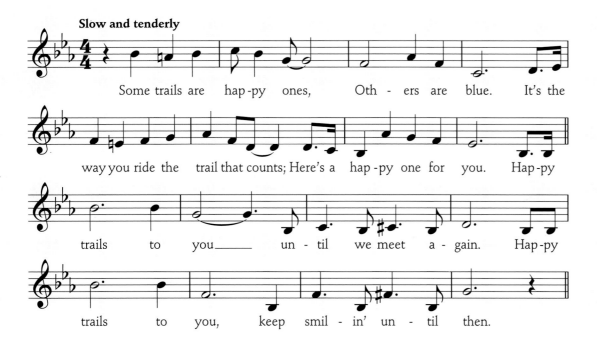

Slow and tenderly

Some trails are hap-py ones, Oth-ers are blue. It's the
way you ride the trail that counts; Here's a hap-py one for you. Hap-py
trails to you___ un-til we meet a-gain. Hap-py
trails to you, keep smil-in' un-til then.

America

BY SAMUEL FRANCIS SMITH (1832)

In 1832, the Reverend Samuel F. Smith wrote new words to the British national anthem, "God Save the King," and produced this popular patriotic anthem.

My country, 'tis of thee,
Sweet land of liberty,
Of thee I sing:
Land where my fathers died,
Land of the Pilgrim's pride,
From every mountainside,
Let freedom ring.

⇒ ACKNOWLEDGMENTS ⇐

We wish to thank the following properties whose cooperation has made this unique collection possible. All care has been taken to trace ownership of these selections and to make a full acknowledgment. If any errors or omissions have occurred, they will be corrected in subsequent editions, provided notification is sent to the compiler.

Front cover—Anonymous, Fourth of July postcard, n.d.

Front flap—Anonymous, colorscrap, circa 1900.

Frontispiece—N. C. Wyeth, *The Pioneers,* 1940.

Title page—R. K. Culver, *The Roosevelt Bears,* 1907.

Preface—Anonymous, lithograph, 1893.

10—Frederic Remington, *The Night Rider,* 1908.

12—Thomas Eakins, *Cowboy Singing,* 1892.

13—Anonymous, *Miss Annie Oakley,* color lithograph poster, 1890.

14—Marsden Hartley, *The Mountain,* 1909.

15—Winslow Homer, *The Veteran in a New Field,* 1865.

16—Warren Davis, untitled, n.d.

17—Anonymous, Union Pacific poster, circa 1910.

18—John Gadsby Chapman, portrait of Davy Crockett, circa 1850. Copyright © Harry Ranson Humanities Research Center, The University of Texas at Austin.

19—F. Boston, *In Lotus Land,* 1900.

20 & 21—Charles M. Russell, *A Mix Up,* 1910.

22—C. N. Wainwright, *Nature's White Mantle,* n.d.

23—Paul Wyttenbach, *Girl With Roses,* color lithograph poster, 1912.

24—Edward H. Potthast, *Children Dancing on the Sand,* 1920.

25—Cecilia Beaux, *Dorothea and Francesca,* 1898.

26—John W. Rader, *Play Ball,* 1925.

27—George Romney, *Portrait of Miss Constable,* 1778.

28 & 29—Norman Rockwell, *Yankee Doodle,* 1937. Reproduced by permission of the Norman Rockwell Family Agency, Inc. Photograph © Bill Bard Associates, Inc., Monticello, NY.

30—P. B. Hicking, untitled, n.d.

31—Berthe Morisot, 1880s.

32—Maurice Prendergast, *Courtyard,* 1901.

33—William McGreger Paxton, *Girl in Sunlight,* 1908.

34—Edmund C. Tarbell, *Racehorse,* circa late 1900s.

36—Childe Hassam, untitled, 1914.

37—J. G. Brown, *The Flower Girl,* 1877.

38—W. H. D. Koerner, *Madonna of the Prairie,* 1921.

39—William Sidney Mount, *Dancing on the Barn Floor,* 1931.

40—Fredrick Morgan, *Sweethearts,* n.d.

41—Anonymous, German postcard, n.d.

43—Frederick C. Friescke, *White Lillies,* 1911.

44—Harry Anderson, untitled, n.d.

45—Charles Predergast, *Fairgrounds,* 1936.

46 & 47—Andrew Wyeth, untitled, n.d.

48—Frank Benson, *Twilight,* 1930.

49—Frances Flora Bond Palmer, Currier & Ives lithograph, 1868.

50—Francis Coutes Jones, *Les Maîtres Contemporains,* 1913.

51—Winslow Homer, *Crossing the Pasture,* 1872.

52—Frederic Remington, *An Arizona Cowboy,* 1901.

53—L. J. Bridgeman, 1900.

54—Frederick Morgan, *Baby,* n.d.

55—Alfred James Rowey, *Spring Moon,* n.d.

56—Anonymous, Fourth of July postcard, circa 1900.

57—Anonymous, German postcard, circa 1880.

59—Thomas Birch, *Sleigh Ride,* 1838.

60—William John Hennessy, *An Old Song,* 1874.

61—Bessie Pease Gutman, *Bubble Pipe,* n.d.

63—Edward Hopper, *Locomotive 177,* 1903.

64—Gene Pressler, *Mary,* 1923.

65—Everett Shinn, *He's the Hobo for Me,* 1945.

66—H. Meserole, *Vogue* cover, n.d.

67—Peter Newell, untitled, 1905.

68 & 69—Anonymous, Fourth of July postcard, n.d.

70—Albert Bierstadt, *Buffalo Head,* 1879.

71—Anonymous, German circus poster, circa 1860.

72—Frederick Edwin Church, *Twilight in the Wilderness,* 1860.

74 & 75—W. H. D. Koerner, *We Been Missing You Something Frightful,* 1925.

76—Eleanor F. Brickdale, *The Gleaners,* 1898.

Back cover—Anonymous, Fourth of July postcard, n.d.